DREAM
apartments

DREAM

apartments

Author

Paco Asensio

Editor

Aurora Cuito

Text

Aurora Cuito:
Minimalist apartment, Energy efficient, Loft in London's Soho, Reconversion of a factory , Attic in São Paulo, Apartment in New York, Apartment beside the Sea, Apartment in San Sadurní, Apartment in Costa San Giorgio, Attic for a publicist, White apartment, Apartment overlooking the Thames, Remodeling of an apartment.

Belén García:
Introduction, Apartment in Manhattan, Dwelling in Barcelona, Apartment for a designer, The L house, The Neisser Residence, The Piper building, Apartment in Belgium, Zen apartment.

Translation

Richard L.Rees

Design

Mireia Casanovas Soley

Layout

Emma Termes

1999 © Loft Publications s.l. and HBI,

an imprint of HarperCollins Publishers

Hardcover ISBN: 0-688-17258-X

Paperback ISBN: 0-8230-6637-1

Printed in Spain

Editorial project:

LOFT publications
Domènec 9, 2 -2
08012 Barcelona. Spain
Tel.: +34 93 218 30 99
Fax: +34 93 237 00 60
e-mail: loft@interplanet.es
www.loftpublications.com

First published in 1999 by **LOFT** and **HBI**,
an imprint of HarperCollins Publishers
10 East 53rd St.
New York, NY 10022-5299

Distributed in the U.S. and Canada
by Watson-Guptill Publications
1515 Broadway
New York, NY 10036
Telephone: (800)-451-1741
(732)- 363-4511 in NJ, AK, HI
Fax: (732)-363-0338

Distributed throughout the rest of the world
by HarperCollins International
10 East 53rd St.
New York, NY 10022-5299

The purpose of *Dream Apartments* is to offer readers an overview of this kind of dwelling, at the threshold of the 21st Century, through a choice selection of projects embracing both architecture and interior design.

The apartments featured in this book, most of which belong to the urban context and reflect a wide variety of needs, clients, authors, and locations, provide a comprehensive sample of city lifestyles. Furthermore, the dwelling is probably one of the architectural forms most sensitive to changes in society, since it responds in an immediate, explicit way to the innermost needs and desires of the individual. And the projects included here are no exception to this rule.

At some stage in their existence, many cities have been on the edge of collapse due to a lack of infrastructures capable of sustaining all the complexities of contemporary life. Traffic congestion, the absence of green zones, the disintegration of the family nucleus, loneliness, noise, and pollution are just some of the factors that make the city an inhospitable place alien to its individual inhabitants.

Parallel to this, and in inverse proportion to the progressive increase in the distance between the city and its citizens, the importance of the dwelling has grown as the center around which the life of city-dwellers revolves. Besides fulfilling its function as a refuge, it is usually a space conceived for one or more individuals, and consequently designed according to their wishes and requirements.

The sacred place of the urbanite, a sheltering haven, an oasis in the midst of chaos, a multi-purpose space in that it offers the possibility of private life and coexistence with others, the dwelling is one of the main identity signs of the human individual in the confusion and anonymity of the metropolis. While neutralizing the effects of uniformity, it provides the individual with a small corner in which to recognize him/herself.

The common denominator of all the apartments featured here is the fact that they are "made-to-measure", in other words, conceived according to the client's personal, family and work circumstances. In some cases, for example, the arrangement of the owners' personal property (paintings, sculptures, objets d'art, or furniture) forms a fundamental part of the project; in others, the apartment becomes a center of operations, in that it is both the client's home and work place.

The versatility that characterizes most of these projects guarantees the apartment-dwellers a certain margin of adaptability, essential when it comes to confronting the insecurity of contemporary life. In some cases, flexibility is even one of the program requirements. This is the case, for example, of the projects that reutilize old buildings and transform them into dwellings.

Dream Apartments offers readers the possibility to "inhabit" some of today's most spectacular apartments and to identify with the desires and aspirations of their creators. In short, to dream.

Location: New York, NY, USA
Photographs: Michael Moran

Apartment with a terrace in Manhattan

Shelton, Mindel & Associates

The first step in the project process followed in this apartment of around 2,160 square feet was to detect those problems that required specific solutions. Thus the following priorities were established: to integrate project and city; to take maximum advantage of the four facades and the roof; and to house a collection of pieces of furniture and objets d'art by 20th Century artists and architects.

On the lower level of the apartment, public and private spaces are very clearly differentiated. The zone most suitable for public relations is organized as from the south facade around an element in the form of a water tank. A large living room with fireplace, and a dining room with an annexed zone in which to sit, are located on either side of the central artifact, a circular space and glass box with a double spiral stainless steel staircase.

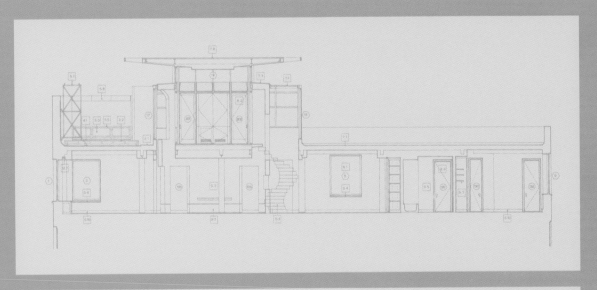

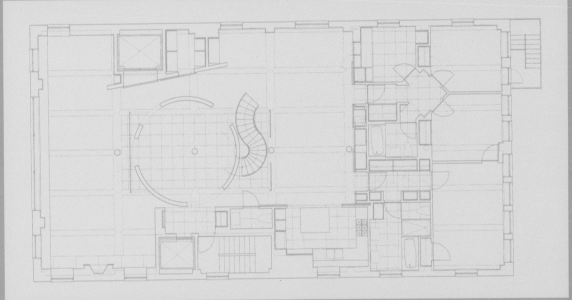

The public and the private, independent

On the west facade, an irregular volume contains the elevator and a storeroom. Furthermore, an L-shaped services strip separates this more public space from the private areas. Part of the L, which contains the vertical communications nucleus, the entrance to the apartment, a toilet, and the kitchen — which opens into the dining room — occupies the east facade. The other part, with a bathroom and dressing room for the two single bedrooms and another for the double bedroom, creates an intermediate zone between bedrooms — with excellent views north — and the rest of the apartment.

In the apartment, the mobile panels acquire a certain importance, since the fact that they may be opened or closed modifies the perception of space. Aluminum, stainless steel, structural white glass, and oak and cherry wood on the floors are some of the materials used for this apartment. Prouvé, Richard Serra, Hoffman, Jacobsen, Aalto, Charles Eames, Caldés, Wagner, and Robert Ryman are some of the artists, sculptors, ceramists, and architects whose works are exhibited inside.

In a single gesture, this new element resolves access to the roof. The enclosed volume makes it possible to link the lower floor — specifically its more public zone — with the roof and the sky, creating a living room on the level above. This volume may also be used as an exhibition space.

Discovering the sky of New York

Shelton, Mindel & Associates have invested all their talents in this apartment for one member of the team, Lee Mindel, as well as all their capacity to detect problems to be faced. Better still, they have found solutions that, apart from working, help to live.

Location: London, UK.
Photographs: Richard Glover.

Minimalist apartment

John Pawson

The term "minimalism" is a very broad one, and over the past ten years it has been much abused and applied to empty, unfinished, weak architecture. While semantically it may admit variations, it encompasses a series of prerequisites that distinguish it from other trends: minimization of formal resources; the use of methods of mathematical composition — such as serialization or repetition —; and above all the will to create a particular work, the meaning of which does not stem from an associated discourse, a creation the meaning of which lies in its striking simplicity.

Of course, there are different types of minimalism. On the one hand, some Mediterranean architects have been refining the legacy of the Modern Movement and the vernacular tradition. On the other, we have the austerity imposed by Calvinism on Central European architecture. Furthermore, contemporary Japanese architecture drinks from the font of the reinterpretation of spiritualism. This latter concept influenced John Pawson during his sojourns in the East.

This British architect shows that only a few gestures may produce powerful designs of quality that need no ornamentation to acquire meaning. Although this is a simple strategy in terms of description, it requires substantial reductionist effort.

The project consists of a succession of monumental walls that articulate the apartment in order to delimit the smaller private rooms. The sober texture of the walls, together with bone-colored tones, constitute a solemn, though warm, finish. The horizontal light bathes the vertical partitions, and the points of light are disguised to avoid direct visual contact.

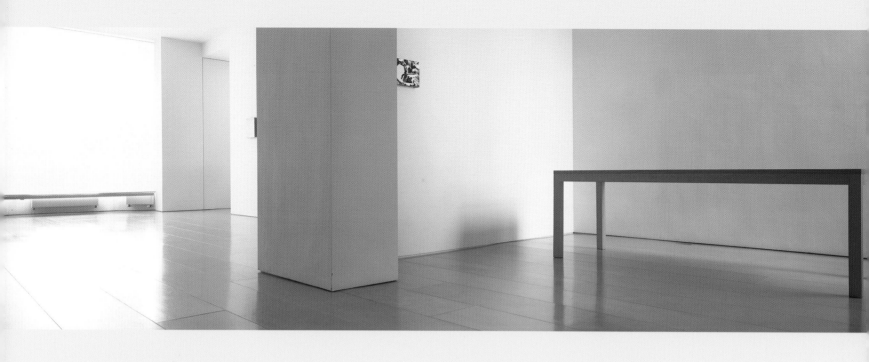

This remodelled apartment is in a Victorian mansion near the Thames. The functional program included a more private area for the living area and a large, open-plan space in which to exhibit works of art. The gallery, the library, and the living space are located at the front. The dining room and kitchen lie behind, linked by a wall about 100 feet long.

Location: Barcelona, Spain.
Photographs: Joan Mundó.

A Dwelling in Barcelona

Franc Fernández

The remodelling of this building transformed what had formerly been a factory-warehouse into a residence. By leaving intact the original height of 14.5 feet, the architect maintained the building's industrial character, at the same time endowing the new apartments with a very marked personality.

Each floor was divided into four spaces of 1,620 square feet. The apartment described here, of 1,190 square feet, is the product of having subdivided one of these. It has the further advantage of occupying a corner of the building, which guarantees natural light throughout. The owner is an actress, which conditioned the kind of space required. Thus, the apartment needed space in which not only to rehearse but also to give performances. Spaciousness, luminosity, and versatility therefore became the priority objectives of the project. The existing structure was respected: the metal pillars and girders, the floor-ceiling structure of ceramic vaults, and even the large original windows. The floor was divided into two zones: on the one hand, and in a single space, the kitchen, dining room, and the living room; and on the other, the bedroom, the bathroom, the toilet, and the studio. The former, the more public of the two, has the original high ceilings and enjoys most of the light penetration. In the latter, however, an intermediate ceiling structure was added that divides the space in half vertically. Beneath this new structure, the more private rooms create a feeling of seclusion and intimacy. Above, an open space 5 feet high accommodates the library. This new floor and the original one below are linked by a wooden staircase.

Exploiting an industrial past

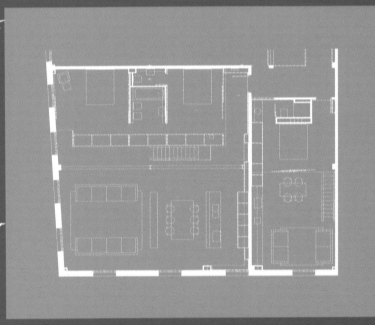

The walls and the ceilings of the apartment have been painted entirely in white, in this way the original structure is highlighted. The outer surface of the volume containing the more private areas has also been painted white. The note of color, however, is to be found on the library floor, on which the beams of light play and from which reflections of the blue industrial paint bounce off in all directions. The floor of the apartment is entirely in solid ipé wood. This, which provides a touch of warmth — very necessary in an apartment of these dimensions — coexists in turn with a decor that emphasizes the building's industrial origins, such as the halogen lamps or the wooden staircase, reminiscent of the ladders used on site.

Luminosity, serenity and intimacy

The volume that contains the bedroom, the bathroom, the toilet, and the studio is clad inside in water-varnished beech wood. The space inside the bathroom is visually increased by mirrors. The rooms are connected by means of sliding doors, some of which are of translucent glass, which means that the square footage of distribution is reduced to a minimum. Franc Fernández has here achieved an apartment in which limited resources were no obstacle to a wealth of solutions. This is further evidence of the fact that a modest budget need never be an excuse for a modest result.

Intelligence and imagination offset a modest budget

Location: London, UK.
Photographs: Andrew Wood / The Interior Archive.

Apartment for a designer

David Edgell

This project stands north of London, in Shoreditch, the center of activities during the nineties of numerous artists and designers of renown, most of them linked to the art trends Cool Britannia and Britart. Old office buildings and warehouses, the prices of which were soaring, have been refurbished and reutilized as studios or apartments. At the same time there has been a proliferation of art galleries, restaurants, and clubs, and a new cinema complex has been created.

David Edgell, a menswear designer, first came to the area in the early nineties, when his company established their offices in Shoreditch. Later, he found in an old Victorian-style gramophone factory the ideal place to live and work: high ceilings, abundant natural light, and an unconventional setting that his clients liked very much. After its refurbishment and subsequent conversion into an apartment — carried out by Edgell himself — the new space provided room for a foyer, an open plan kitchen-living room, a room in which to keep dirty dishes and to wash clothes, a studio with a fireplace, a bedroom, and a bathroom. Edgell's wish to enhance the sensation of space and to keep his plans as open as possible was partially frustrated by Britain's severe fire regulations, which forced him to add a number of partitions to the original structure. These, as well as the doors, were carefully designed so that small shadow lines at their ends — one next to the ceiling and the other next to the floor — highlighted the independence of these elements from the floor-ceiling structures.

The furniture was chosen with extraordinary loving care, for this is one of Edgell's weaknesses (his bookshelf, next to the studio fireplace, contains many volumes on this subject). Art-nouveau armchairs, a stainless steel kitchen unit, lamps that create a semi-industrial atmosphere, and chairs by 20th Century designers (a red plastic chair by Charles Eames in the studio and pastel-toned ones by Arne Jacobsen around the dining-room table) coexist harmoniously in this apartment.

The electrical installation is under the parquet floors, on the surface of which different sockets have been placed to enhance functional versatility.

Outstanding among the new textures and colors are the very light blues and moss greens applied to the walls as an alternative to clinical white, and the unique greenish slate cladding in part of the bathroom.

Edgell's project is deceivingly simple, since his apparently austere apartment has managed to absorb the complexity of everyday life in London on the threshold of the 21st Century.

Designed simplicity

The L House

Sauerbruch & Hutton

Location: London, UK.
Photographs: Michael Claus, Katsuhisa Kida, Helène Binet, Charlie Stebbings.

Sauerbruch & Hutton were required to remodel this old, conventional, Victorian semi-detached house in London. The building, the four floors of which total a surface area of around 1,836 square feet, was redesigned to contain offices on the first two and a dwelling on the remaining two above. The clients in this case were the architects themselves. The reconversion work revealed how the concept of space — or of mentality, which amounts to the same thing — had evolved from Victorian times to the early nineties, when the project was executed. During the latter half of the 19th Century, building interiors were usually divided into many closed, centripetal spaces. In contrast, at the end of the 20th Century the trend is to obtain practical, open, diaphanous space in which there is often an interplay — visual and physical — between the different zones of the project and the project and its surroundings. With minimal gestuality, Sauerbruch & Hutton have achieved excellent results. After a vertical itinerary in which sensations increase in intensity as we climb, the climax is reached precisely on the top floor: all partitions having been eliminated, the floor is completely open plan, and the living room, the dining room, and the kitchen constitute a single space. All this beneath a totally glazed gable roof that replaces the original structure.

The decision to open the building through the roof — a triumph in these latitudes, where natural light is scarce — places the project in contact with a unique, ever-changing and enormously attractive landscape: the London sky. The celestial vault is thus converted into a kind of extension of the dwelling, a private "garden". During the day, natural light floods the interior, either directly or filtered through curtains. On the other hand, at dusk a column of artificial light rises up from this top floor to be lost, creating a theatrical effect, in the darkness of the night.

The use of color and textures is a further characteristic of this project. Bright colors, warm wood surfaces, and fine cladding endow this apartment with a high degree of comfort. A perfect example of Sauerbruch & Hutton's intelligence and spirit of sensuality when it comes to reinterpreting — imposing their own character on — an existing space.

The celestial garden

The project is partially characterized by the search for balance between functionalism, the need for privacy, and free flow from one space to the next. In this context, the strategic placing of cupboards plays a fundamental role, since in this way storage space is restricted to specific areas, freeing the rest of the floor. On the one hand, we find cupboards all along the perimeter, taking advantage of the outer wall recesses; on the other, they appear as separating elements between rooms, rather like partitions.

Location: Chicago, Illinois.
Photographs: Hedrich Blessing.

The Neisser Residence

Tigerman McCurry Architects

Shortly after having become widowed, Judith Neisser, a freelance writer, commissioned Stanley Tigerman and Margaret I. McCurry to remodel this apartment of around 3,780 square feet in Chicago. On the 62nd floor of the Kohn Pederson & Fox Complex, at the end of the Magnificent Mile, the large facade surfaces guarantee privileged views of the city from practically every room. Tigerman and McCurry attempted to maintain the succession of multiple closed spaces into which the apartment was originally divided — each one with a specific use and well communicated, visually and physically, to each other — instead of opting for the popular, multi-purpose open-plan spaces. Moreover, they carried out meticulous recovery work on the exiting floor-ceiling structures by deviating the drainpipes — formerly rather badly placed — by either embedding them in the structure itself or in the party walls, thus re-establishing the unusual distance between the structures of just over eleven feet.

The ground plan reflects the intention to create closed, independent spaces related to the adjacent environments, through the use of transparent partitions or direct accesses.

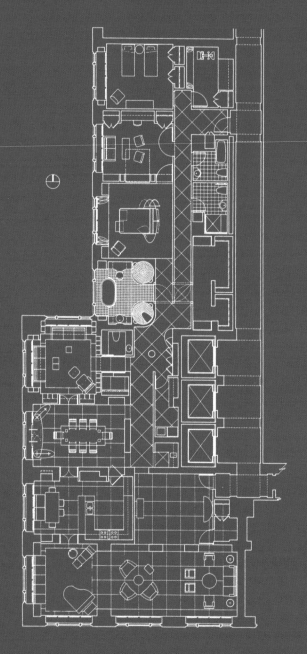

Paradoxically, by minimizing details in this apartment, its architecture is highlighted, and the deliberately empty space recovers something of its original character, its essence.

Absences and presences. Chicago in sight

A progression of closed spaces

Tigerman and McCurry have come up with a made-to-measure apartment for their client, through dialogue and collaboration with her. Spaces of great privacy alternate with other spaces suitable for intense social life. The architects' efforts here were endorsed by many years of experience, which have been justly rewarded with the Chicago AIA interior decoration award.

Location: Vienna, Austria.
Photographs: Andreas Wagner, Margherita Spiluttini.

Energy efficient apartment

Lichtblau & Wagner

The reconversion of this attic in Vienna is characterized by the application of energy-saving ideas hitherto adapted only to other architectural domains. While in residential architecture the main concerns were functional or aesthetic aspects, Lichtblau & Wagner have introduced concepts of energy efficiency and economy into this field. In order to achieve energy saving, these young Austrian architects have ruled out all superficial luxuries, marble bathrooms, pointless terraces, and grandiose entrances to concentrate on a flexible project that economizes on energy, budget, and space. Four basic units were conceived of 540 square feet each, organized in pairs and with an additional space that may be added to one apartment or the other. This alteration is easy to achieve thanks to the simple relocation of partitions. The common spaces house a storeroom, a laundry, and a multi-purpose space for meetings or parties, which offsets the lack of space in the studios.

The project offers flexibility in the use of space. The available surface area is maximum, since circulation zones have been eliminated. The different areas may be used for different activities during the day and throughout the year. The maximum exponent of this idea is the space beneath sliding windows, since depending on the weather, it may be used as a terrace, a gallery, or a greenhouse. Curtains separate this space thermally from the rest of the dwelling, and create a sensation of warmth and comfort.

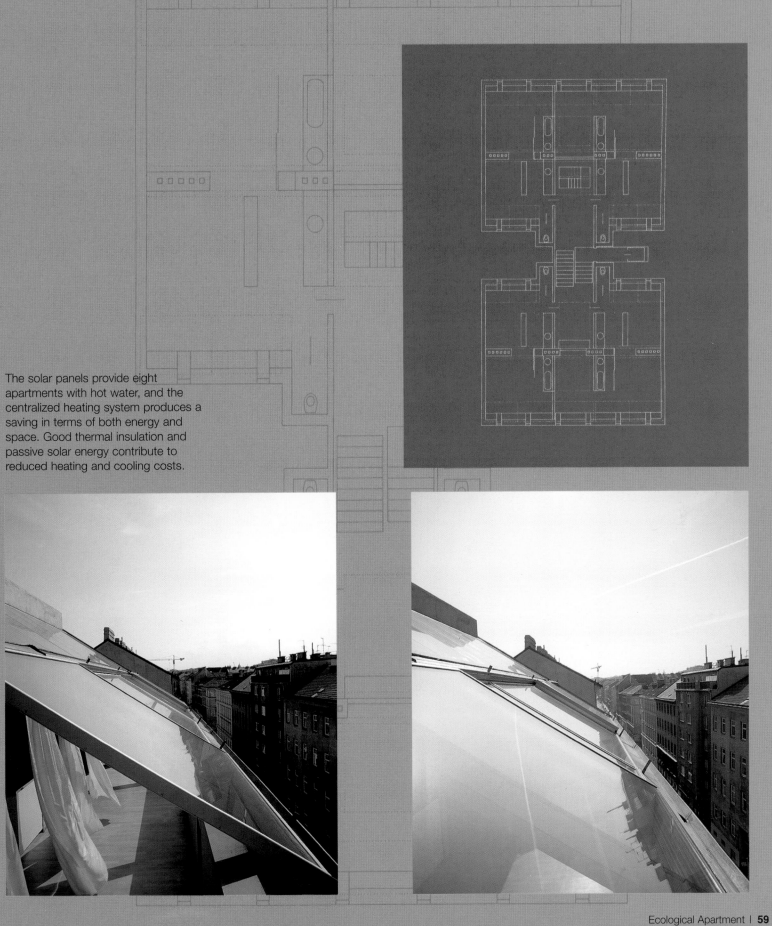

The solar panels provide eight apartments with hot water, and the centralized heating system produces a saving in terms of both energy and space. Good thermal insulation and passive solar energy contribute to reduced heating and cooling costs.

From the constructional point of view, the absence of interior walls contributes to reducing costs. Moreover, the installations are in the floor, thus obviating the need for sockets in the vertical partitions. The kitchen and bathroom units are collapsible, and are connected to the drains through holes in the flooring. In this way, their positions may be interchanged, or they may simply be removed when not needed.

Litchtblau & Wagner's bathrooms are linked to the living areas. They are not conceived as hermetic units, they are lit by natural light, and from them it is possible to view the daytime areas.

The Piper Building

Lifschutz Davidson

The transformation of the Gas Corporation Research Centre
building by Lifschutz Davidson is a good example of how,
with intelligence and constancy, it is possible to transfer the
client's dreams to paper.

Parallel to the announcement that this early sixties

The reconversion of the building has left very few traces of its immediate past. The first is the distance between floor-ceiling structures of 13 feet in the apartments, the skilfull exploitation of which resulted in the design of double-height living areas. Another, the large dimensions of the windows, simplified the composition of the facade and maximized the penetration of the weak light of London. A sign of adaptation to the new residential use is the incorporation of balconies, sustained by a metallic structure anchored to the roof.

Access to the apartments is almost invariably from the passages that link the vertical nuclei. When we enter one, we discover that while the first zone we encounter usually has a distributive and services function, the dining room, living room, and bedrooms all look outwards through the large windows. For their part, the stairs and kitchen help to define the space vertically.

Flexibility and respect

High-tech on the human scale

Another feature is the discriminate use of colors and materials, which contrast sharply with the white of facades and interiors. Thus, while the parquet provides warmth, bright tones highlight specific aspects of the project.

The Piper Building is a further example of Lifschutz Davidson's respect for and commitment to his client, program, and site. Something very difficult to achieve when exercising what is known as ethical architecture.

Location: Koksidje, Belgium.
Photographs: Jan Verlinde.

Apartment in Belgium

Non Kitch Group

Non Kitch Group, a young Belgian team working in the fields not only of architecture but also of interior and furniture design, was set up in 1995, fruit of the association between architect L. Arschoot and artist William Sweetlove. The fact that they come from different — though linked — professional fields has generated a common ground in which points of view and influences are mixed and mutually enriched. This apartment is a good example of N.K.G.'s architectural vision, in which art ceases to be an "a posteriori" addition to become an essential part of the space. Eclectic and easy-going, they define their works as the result of an original blend of minimalism and the "Memphis style". This 2,050 square-foot apartment occupies the top two floors of a building. The two floors below similarly accommodate another apartment of the same dimensions, while part of the ground floor is occupied by two garages, one for each dwelling. The building shares a party wall with the one next door, which means that the three remaining facades are freed. On the other hand, the need to adapt to a narrow 19.5-foot span was a decisive consideration when it came to organizing the ground plan. Thus, both the entrance to the building in one half, and the staircase, which is annexed to the access area, minimize distribution surfaces and make it possible to take full advantage of the narrow construction.

Dining room: chairs by Philip
Starck. Kitchen: table by N.K.G.,
painting by William Sweetlove
(1996), African mask from the
exhibition "Magicien de la terre",
"Paris" lamp by Sottsass, Andy
Warhol Campbell's soup cans.

Art becomes part
of the space

Another resource applied to achieve the sensation of greater space was the displacement of part of each floor with respect to the rest. This simple operation spectacularly increased the spatial richness by visually linking several rooms and thus opening different perspectives inside the dwelling. The apartment, now on four levels thanks to this displacement, has the kitchen and dining room on level 3, three bedrooms, bathroom and toilet on level 4, a study and part of a double space over the dining room on level 5, and a living room giving onto a terrace with views of the dune landscape, and an area annexed to the room in which to watch television, on level 6.

The displacement of part of each floor with respect to the rest increases the spatial richness.

In this apartment, N.K.G. worked with an architecture closely linked to art. Thus, the white-painted walls both achieve an increase in luminosity and create a neutral backdrop against which to place the many works by artists and designers (including Joseph Beuys, Roy Lichtenstein, Mario Merz, Christo, Andy Warhol, Mendini, Di Rosa, Rosi, Philip Starck, Sottsass, Sipek, and E. Cucci). Even the heating and the lighting are placed to enhance the artworks, evidence of the fact that with N.K.G. the links between architecture and art are subject to constant re-examination and redefinition.

Living room: "Richard II" chair, Philip Starck; "Lola Mundo" chair, Philip Starck; "Louis 20" chair, Philip Starck; oil drum by Christo; chaise-longue by Le Corbusier; Mendira table. Photograph: Cindy Sherman; litho: Enzo Cucci; litho: Tom Wesselman.

Location: London, UK.
Photographs: Simon Archer.

Reconversion of a factory

Simon Conder Associates

The need for open space, without any form of compartmentalization, governed this project in a former factory. The client, a painter living in Kent, needed an apartment in London as her base of operations, in order to exploit the artistic life of the capital. The objective was to take maximum advantage of a 1,250 square foot extension by potentiating the sense of space and the luminosity that characterized the original property. This decision overrode the partition of space, although not in detriment to effective functionalism.

Given the scarcity of available surface area, it was decided that the apartment would consist of one single space, visually divided by the stairs that separate the living area from the bedroom. Three vertical elements define the main area: the stainless steel stove, and two cylinders that house the shower and a toilet. The party walls have a number of functions: they contain the cupboards, the installations, and even a folding bed for guests with its corresponding toilet.

The materials used in the project confer a certain minimalist air onto the ambience. The stove, the stair structure, and the profiles in the glazed gallery are of stainless steel. The flooring is of white oak and contains the heating.

Open space versus functionalism

The success of this project, by a team of English architects, lies in the fact that superficial or ornamental elements that would spoil its clarity were ruled out. The installations are concealed in ceilings, cupboards and furniture. In this way, independent light points became unnecessary. The translucent cylinders, for example, are lit by skylights during the day. At night, they radiate artificial light that illuminates the whole apartment.

The brilliance of the project lies in its apparent simplicity

The furniture, except for the dining-room chairs by Wegner Wishbone, was also designed by Simon Conder Associates. All the pieces were conceived as mobile units with artificial light incorporated.

The central section of the apartment is of double height, which makes access possible to the terrace on the floor above. The studio, oriented toward London's West End, enjoys views of the city to the south and west.

Location: London ,UK.
Photographs: Jefferson Smith, Laurent Kalfala, Knott Architects.

Loft in London's Soho

Knott Architects

The empty shell of a loft may cause consternation among many clients. Open spaces with no functional differentiation and underestimation of available space mean that some potential purchasers are easily put off. The result of such fear is often the wish to divide the loft into traditional rooms, which spoils its spatial potential.

Knott Architects were faced with the challenge of fitting two bedrooms, two bathrooms, a kitchen, and a living room into 1,296 square feet in a refurbished building in London's Soho. The success of their endeavour, without compromising the integrity of the space, is thanks to a stringent design philosophy, which makes a clear, permanent distinction between inserted elements and the containing shell.

The bedrooms are understood as pieces of furniture that touch neither the ceiling nor the party walls, except on the glazed edges of the partitions. All interventions are in wood, steel, and glass, thus distinguishing the new construction from the existing walls, plastered and painted white. The partitions are highlighted by a wooden dais that covers the entire floor and conceals the installations beneath.

Flows of light and air

The floors and the service strip that runs along the whole length of the apartment are in maple. On the other hand, the partitions do not disguise the versatility of plywood, showing it exactly as it is. Constructional details have been scrupulously conceived, and include the visible fixing elements, the exposed edges of wooden boards, and the shadows cast by interruptions between materials. All these details together constitute an integral structure.

Location: Xàbia, Spain.
Fhotographs: Eugeni Pons.

The remodeling of an apartment

Salvador Villalba

The truly brilliant aspect of this project by Salvador Villalba is its apparent simplicity. The obstacles he has had to overcome are disguised in the form of constructional details that enrich the perception of space without complicating it. The remodeling of this apartment in Xàbia (Javea) includes the design of many of the pieces of furniture, the installation of a new system of artificial lighting, and the creation of a new building system that governs the layout.

Outstanding among the interventions is the treatment of the vertical partitions: while some have simply been painted or stuccoed, others have been clad in wood to endow the interior with a greater feeling of warmth. Still others, like the one in the living room, are of double thickness in order to accommodate installations and pieces of furniture encrusted in the wall. This

Location: São Paulo, Brazil.
Photographs: Tuca Reinés.

Attic in
São Paulo

Arthur de Mattos Casas

The work of Arthur de Mattos Casas encompasses many disciplines, so it is hard to gauge the extent of the influence of his creative activity. Just like a man of the Renaissance — artist, architect, craftsman, and philosopher, a hunter of ideas — this versatile Brazilian strives to achieve a solid, coherent relationship between space and the objects that occupy it. And what better way to achieve this than designing both elements? On the one hand, the place, and on the other, the utensils that serve the needs of this space, both functionally and visually. The interior design process in this and other projects by de Mattos Casas is marked by a counterpoint between the purity of rationalism and the sumptuousness of decoration. Rationalism defends formal essence against ornament. This apartment is evidence of the fact that both trends may exist harmoniously side-by-side. The merit lies in having unified them into a single concept, in having designed objects the essence of which allows a certain poetic licence in details.

Architecture, design and craftwork

This apartment in Sao Paulo occupies the top two floors of a building. Consequently, it enjoys magnificent views over the city. The dining room and living room are closed to the exterior by means of a mesh of wooden slats, which protects the interior from direct sunlight and provides greater privacy. The lighting is one of the most carefully conceived elements of the project. Warm, uniform light was designed, together with points of light that bring certain places to the fore, either for functional reasons or else to feature an object or work of art.

Inlaid work and the use of different types of wood, for both structural and ornamental elements, return here. The stairs joining the two levels are an example of renovation in the use of wood. This piece consists of steps in the form of drawers, the structural raison d'être of which lies in the way each one rests on the one below. In this way an almost sculptural object of extreme elegance is obtained.

The kitchen and bathrooms are the product of simple, forceful design. The effort to minimize complicated forms contributes to the fact that the more functional parts of the apartment are extremely practical, while retaining their identity and harmonizing with the overall style.

Poetic details

Location: Milan, Italy.
Photographs: Interstampa.

Zen apartment

This apartment is a curious alternative within the range of possibilities available to architects and designers. With elements manufactured almost entirely in the West, an environment more characteristic of Japan than of Europe has been created, in terms both of spatial experience and of the kind of visual images featured.

The functional organization of this almost square apartment of some 970 square feet is at first sight simple. A wall divides it into two, separating the daytime from the nighttime zones. Access to the apartment is gained from the nighttime zone, beyond which lies its daytime equivalent. Left behind to the right are the master bedroom and the large bathroom and, to the left, the guest room (which can be used as a meditation room when there are no guests). In the daytime zone, and annexed to the guest room, we find the kitchen and a toilet, opposite which stands the living-dining room.

This clear division into different spaces is tempered by differences in level — between the bathroom and the bedroom, and between the dining and living areas — and by the presence of movable panels or shoji, which act as interior walls that in a single gesture isolate certain spaces from or communicate them with the rest of the dwelling. The fact that these panels are made of traditional parchment means that even when they are closed they allow a degree of visual communication, thanks to their translucent quality.

The attractive decor, which was studied down to the last detail, was achieved with furniture and elements — mostly from the West — in the oriental style. Compagnie Française de l'Orient, Marco Polo, On Futon, Gervasoni, and Artemide are only a few of the creators and distributors who have contributed to this curious final result.

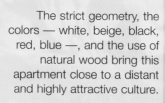

The strict geometry, the colors — white, beige, black, red, blue —, and the use of natural wood bring this apartment close to a distant and highly attractive culture.

The advantages of Japanese culture now also in the West

Alterations to an apartment in the Eixample

Bercedo + Mestre

Location: Barcelona, Spain.
Photographs: Eugeni Pons.

This project consists of alterations to a 1,026 square-foot apartment (plus a terrace of 130 square feet) in Barcelona's Eixample district, for one occupier. Like many apartments in the area, its characteristics are typical of those of the first decades of this century. On the one hand, it features highly attractive elements: ceilings with timber beams and hand-made vaults; considerable height between floor-ceiling structures; and large doors of wood and glass. On the other, it presents obvious defects: an obsolete distribution; clear disproportion between the depth (75 feet) and width (16 feet) of the dwelling; restricted entry of natural light at the ends; and ventilation of the rooms by means of badly lit inner patios. Consequently, the architects adopted a twofold strategy: first, to enhance the presence of the more valuable elements, either by removing false ceilings or widening the views; second, to study ways to transform defects into qualities.

Potentiate advantages, reduce drawbacks

The first decision was to demolish all the existing partitions, since the very depth of the apartment established a polarity between one end of the apartment and the other. In this way, differentiation between uses and different degrees of privacy was established not through real divisions but through distance. The itinerary leading from the daytime to the nighttime zones, from private to shared areas, became the system by which the different environments of the dwelling are interrelated.

The wall is demolished

Similarly, the natural light from the two ends of the apartment is transmitted by a system of transparencies: translucent glass panes that link spaces such as the study and the master bedroom, or the living room and the kitchen, without there being a direct relationship between them.

Around the recesses formed by the tiny inner patios, in the middle of the dwelling, stand the kitchen, a bathroom, and a toilet. In this way, the itinerary through the apartment acquires an S-shape which avoids a direct visual relationship between the daytime and nighttime zones. At the point of inflection, the ceiling has been lowered and the corridor has been narrowed to a minimal width, which acts as a counterpoint to the spaciousness of the remaining environments.

1. Kitchen
2. Dinning room
3. Toilet
4. Bathroom
5. Bedroom
6. Wardrobe
7. Living room

The shower and toilet stand where the apartment narrows due to the presence of the entrance and the small inner patio. Gresite provides a fresh, summery environment.

Location: New York, NY, USA.
Photographs: Dennis Krukowski.

Apartment in New York

Tony Foy

The world of interior design constitutes an ambiguous field of research that may be approached from a wide variety of perspectives. The relationship between an individual and his/her immediate surroundings has existed since the advent of mankind, and may be interpreted in many different ways. Outstanding among recent innovations are variations in the section of the project: different horizontal and vertical levels appear that enrich space and help toward its definition. On the other hand, and also in relation to the delimitation of environments, another way of understanding vertical partitions has emerged. Walls have ceased to be impenetrable barriers to become flexible, mobile, even invisible elements.

Finally, we observe how design is no longer an anonymous process (although it may still occasionally be an amateur one), rather the product of a creator who endows his environments with a particular personality. Such specialization is revealed in the world of furniture, which in recent years has become the fruit of exclusive design. Hence the fact that decor has become the simple positioning of individual elements in a room, often regardless of the specificity of space and its intrinsic potential. The project featured on these pages is an example of how furniture may endow space with character without altering its original characteristics. The apartment contains pieces by different designers, even belonging to different eras and styles, and yet the effect is one of astonishing homogeneity that transforms the rooms into a feast for the senses.

The tonal neutrality of most of the elements in the living room enhances the magnificently colorful views at sunset. Thanks to the position of the windows and their discreet carpentry, the views resemble framed paintings.

The light tones of walls and floors act as the ideal backdrop to dark furniture and colorful objects. At the same time, flowers and plants add a further touch of life to the environment.

Individual points of illumination that highlight specific objects, which may be either works of art or areas in which to read or have a meal, offset the overall uniform lighting.

Location: Knokke-le-Zoete, Belgium.
Photographs: Mihail Moldoveanu.

Apartment beside the Sea

Gaetano Pesce

In a building by the sea, in the Belgian town of Knokke-le-Zoete,
Robbie Mourmans' apartment is a fascinating artistic adventure
on which the architect-designer Gaetano Pesce embarked in
1994. The common denominator of Pesce's latest interior
designs is concrete, although the final appearance of his
projects is the result of an astonishing mixture of paints, resins,
and flooring conceived and personalized by the artist and his
team of collaborators. These materials are the product of
meticulous chemical trials to test their durability and stability in
specific climatic conditions. His predilection for synthetic
materials is the fruit of ecological convictions. In the words of
Pesce himself: "I prefer to use the most horrible of plastics
rather than wood, to prevent the disappearance of entire
forests". The discovery of new materials governs most of his

In this apartment, all the spaces are endowed with very different atmospheres. The kitchen, which opens into the living room, enjoys magnificent views of the sea, and contains exclusive furniture that create a surrealist, though comfortable, atmosphere. The cupboards in the daytime zone are of different heights and consist of panels of painted resin. When lit at night, they recall the braziers of the past.

The bedrooms are the product of eccentricity. The master bedroom is separated from the daytime zones by a door featuring the stylized silhouette of the owner. The bed is presided over by the illustration of a couple embracing. The guest room consists of a bed-cupboard that opens threateningly like the metaphor of a huge mouth about to engulf its victims. The wardrobe doors are also of resin, and feature drawings of enormous articles of clothing.

The apartment is crammed with details, winks of the eye, tricks, corners designed to create ingenious, ever-changing, and almost invariably astonishing environments. Gaetano Pesce insists on creating furniture and spaces that make each project unique. Far from neutrality, his designs are true works of multidisciplinary art.

Location: Sant Sadurní, Spain.
Photographs: Eugeni Pons.

Apartment in Sant Sadurní

Josep Juvé

In this apartment, architecture and decoration combine to form a complex, functional space. Both disciplines were reflected on simultaneously, so it is difficult to decide whether the different elements are the consequence of a structural, functional, or purely formal requirement. Essence and ornament cannot be disassociated, and are necessary to endow the dwelling with meaning.

The development of the project was based on field work closely linked to improvisation. However, this does not mean that decisions were taken randomly, but rather that work progressed on the basis of previously chosen alternatives. Observation of what had been built nourished the new designs. Besides the building itself and the furniture, special attention was paid to the finishes, specifically on painting. All the corners enjoy exclusive tones that highlight different details. The wall lamps, for example, stand out against the rest of the vertical partitions. On the other hand, some of the walls feature inscriptions that play a twofold role: one semantic and the other visual. Similarly, the paint serves to falsify textures. Thus brick is dissolved in different pastel shades, while wood disappears behind gilt.

Poetics and imagination

The originality of this project lies in it sincerity. No devices were used to disguise installations, and surfaces were treated to accentuate textures, and the cupboards reveal their contents, since only a few have doors. The perception of space, although rather chaotic, is frank and spontaneous.

Without complexes

Even the staircase changes in nature as it climbs. The first step is of wood, a kind of introduction, and this is followed by a pair of masonry steps that confer solidity on the structure. Further up, the steps become malleable metal sheets that folds until the wooden mezzanine is reached. This element is a compendium of ideas that govern the project: a mixture of constructional details, materials, colors, textures and finishes that form a heterogeneous ensemble, producing a multitude of sensations that enrich perception of the ambience.

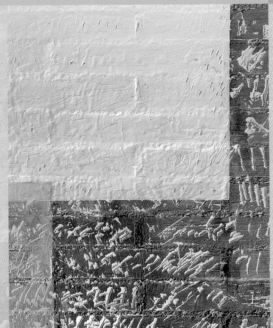

The illumination presents a number of different solutions. On the one hand, natural light enters through windows that vary in terms of transparency: the panes of treated glass differ in texture and opacity. On the other, there are numerous lamps: some standing on the floor and giving off a diffuse light; others are table lamps; and still others are "festival" lights purely for decoration, since the light they give off is merely referential.

Location: Florence, Italy.
Photographs: Alessandro Ciampi.

House in Costa San Giorgio

Studio Archea

To intervene in old buildings is invariably a complex task. If the quality of the existing structure is doubtful, the best solution is to start from scratch. Restoration is never economically profitable, since it carries with it the need for a series of preliminary decisions and requires much time for conceptual thought. A preliminary study must be conducted of the site and period of the original construction. These reflections influence the decision to refurbish some elements, while leaving other parts as they are. Furthermore, restoration requires almost specific building techniques for each detail.

Italian architects have always shone in this field, since their rich architectural past has provided them with the opportunity to constantly research and practise. A good example of this "savoir faire" is the apartment designed by Studio Archea, near the Ponte Vecchio in the heart of Florence.

The original building is renaissance, and features large wooden beams that endow it with a certain majestic quality. The challenge was to design a dwelling that would exploit the exceptional qualities of the Quattrocento, while at the same time creating a functional, contemporary environment.

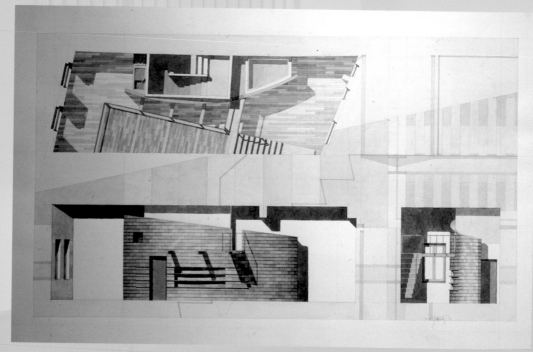

Author design

Given the limited dimensions of the project, the architects had the opportunity to design all the elements in detail. In this way they avoided prefabrication and produced unique, almost sculptural, objects. A fine example of this is Studio Archea's design of the iron staircase that leads up to the mezzanine, made by Modulo Laser, the firm also responsible for the kitchen, the stone wall, and the timber flooring.

The space is arranged around a curvilinear stone wall that articulates the different functions of the dwelling and constitutes the support for the metal girders on which the mezzanine nighttime zone rests. From this horizontal platform, a small panoramic swimming pool is reached by crossing a bridge.

A house on the coast

Tono Lledó

Location: Moraira, Spain.
Photographs: Eugeni Pons.

This project stands on a magnificent enclave on the coast of Alicante, just above the quarry the stone from which was formerly used to build local houses. The house enjoys splendid views of the sea and the majestic Peñón de Ifach. The house forms part of a complex of eight dwellings, and was conceived on the basis of two apartments on different floors. The spaces are arranged around the staircase that forms a large central void and acts as the nexus between both levels. It is the element that endows the project with cohesion and endows the distribution with meaning. Furthermore, its structure of steel and Burmese teak transform it into a sculptural object.

The original architecture was radically transformed. The main aim here was to create a sensation of spaciousness and to establish a close relationship between the exteriors and views and the interior. From the very outset, the architect sought a perfect symbiosis between space, light, and color. The refined tastes of the owner and his special interest in matters of design contributed much to Tono Lledó's work.

The top floor accommodates the kitchen, a small toilet, and the living-dining room, which is divided into three large spaces. The terrace, on the same floor, has a light, almost minimalist, appearance, in order not to obstruct the magnificent views of the sea.

A symbiosis between space, light, and color

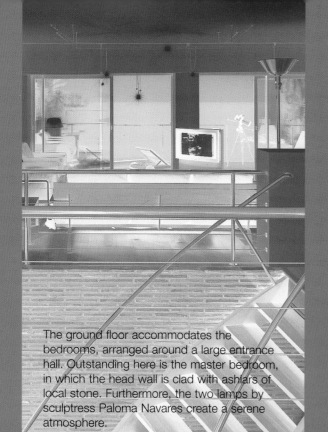

The project is a meticulous, sophisticated work of design, including the highly appropriate choice of materials, furniture and lighting, in which the owner had an enormously important role to play.

The ground floor accommodates the bedrooms, arranged around a large entrance hall. Outstanding here is the master bedroom, in which the head wall is clad with ashlars of local stone. Furthermore, the two lamps by sculptress Paloma Navares create a serene atmosphere.

The materials and textures used on the wall faces vary practically from room to room: stucco, brick, and travertine marble, among others. Although the residential complex is perfectly in keeping with its maritime setting, it is isolated from the exterior by a rubblework wall, the work of the much solicited local masons.

Location: São Paulo.
Photographs: Tuca Reinés.

Attic for a publicist

Arthur de Mattos Casas

The apartment occupies the two top floors of a São Paulo building, and was designed for a famous publicist. Due to the fact that the number of occupants fluctuates, the dwelling was divided into three different zones. In the first place, the area for the children, who sporadically occupy these rooms. This includes the bedrooms and a room for the television and computer. This same floor accommodates the living area, the salon, dining room, kitchen, and wash place. The floor above houses the client's private quarters, joined to a terrace with swimming pool. The project involved no conceptual effort as far as domestic programs are concerned. Efforts here were directed toward placing different works of art and collector's pieces. The main objective was that all these elements should be placed flexibly, without cluttering space, altering it while also embellishing it. Hence the fact that the pictures are hung from rails by steel cables that may be easily displaced. Furthermore, the objects were put into display cabinets so that they would not obstruct the overall visual effect and be highlighted as they deserve, thanks to specific protection and lighting in each case.

The staircase linking both floors consists of a white-painted metal structure to which wooden steps were attached. Although the materials and finishes coincide with those of the dwelling, this element appears sculptural and confers character on the space.

The wood and glass display cases are the solution to the problem of storage and exhibition of valuable objects. Thanks to these elements, it was possible to display the objects in all their splendour while preserving their fragility. The initial objective was not to clutter tables and sideboards, leaving them free for other functions.

Arthur de Mattos Casas' studio not only conceives architectural spaces but also produces some of the furniture elements for the project, in this case the rug and the dining-room table. The apartment also contains design pieces: the dining-room chairs are by Charles Eames, the lamp by Pierre Chareau, and the sofa by Jean Michel Frank.

The client's private quarters have a landscaped terrace with views of the city. Due to the weight that the structure supporting the swimming pool and the plants had to bear, it had to be considerably reinforced. The studio on this level contains a fireplace, an office, and a bookcase.

Location: London, UK.
Photographs: Richard Glover.

Apartment in white

Arthur Collin

White interior spaces are a commonplace, a custom, a convenience. White is the chromatic base par excellence, neutrality. Aware of this, Arthur Collin has designed an apartment in which white not only predominates, but it is also the absolute protagonist, multi-functional and solicitous. Based on the fact that there is no single white, the project emphasizes the subtle differences between three different whites. Unlike the cold effect of minimalist white, the variations between these tones endow the dwelling with warmth. The apartment is the result of the remodelling of an attic in a Georgian building. The house was totally altered in the seventies, so it became possible to insert an entirely contemporary interior without coming across original elements of a certain historical value.

The main objectives of the project were to create flexible space; large, luminous interiors; and flowing links between all the rooms. The strategy to unify all the related environments consisted of conceiving furniture in different

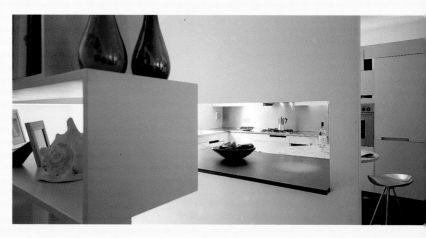

The living room cupboards are extended until they reach the kitchen, where they accommodate the appliances. This piece of furniture unites the two spaces, although the composition of the doors endows each zone with its own character. The handles are slots, so that the surface, though smooth and monolithic, is seen to be geometrical and textured.

The kitchen consists of an L-shaped unit that includes the sink and the stainless steel hood. The folding table is of recycled plastic, a mixture of detergent bottles that may be appreciated in the different tones of the surface.

The bookcase on the stairs is an ingenious mechanism consisting of thirteen old boxes painted in three tones of white. Thanks to this mechanism, there was no need to build bannisters.

With this project, Arthur Collin shows that such a common basic, color as white is capable of endowing a space with character. This London architect has carried the use of white to the limit, and the result is a comfortable, warm, entirely contemporary home.

Location: London, UK.
Photographs: Claudio Silvestrin Architects.

Apartment overlooking the Thames

Claudio Silvestrin

The formal purity of a building makes it possible to focus attention on other aspects: the furniture, the materials, the finishes, the light, views, and so on. Claudio Silvestrin's objective here was precisely this: to emphasize certain aspects of the dwelling through the neutralisation of forms. The apartment is austere, sober, almost minimalist, and endows space with the virtue of disappearing behind elements that were designed to stand out. In this way materials acquire multiple functions: besides configuring the final image of the project, they highlight the panoramic views of the city, which are reflected on their surfaces. A further distinguishing feature of the dwelling are the efforts made to disguise the installations. A multitude of details conceal technology to potentiate the almost Calvinistic abstraction of the project. The devices needed to make the apartment function are placed behind glazed screens, behind vertical partitions, or behind the cupboard doors. For example, the heating is beneath the flooring, together with sound-absorbing material.

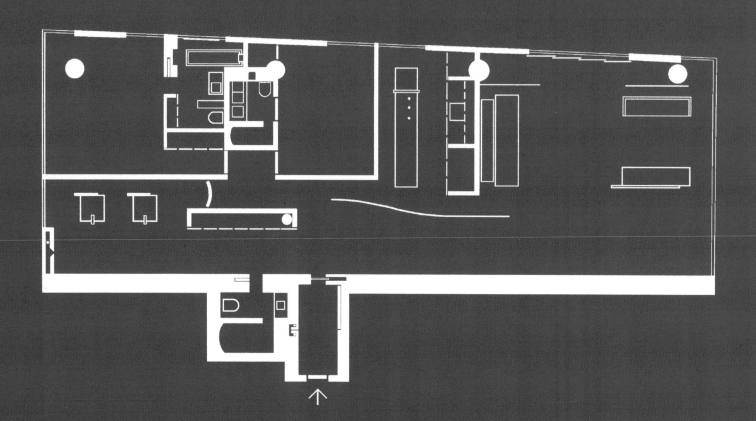

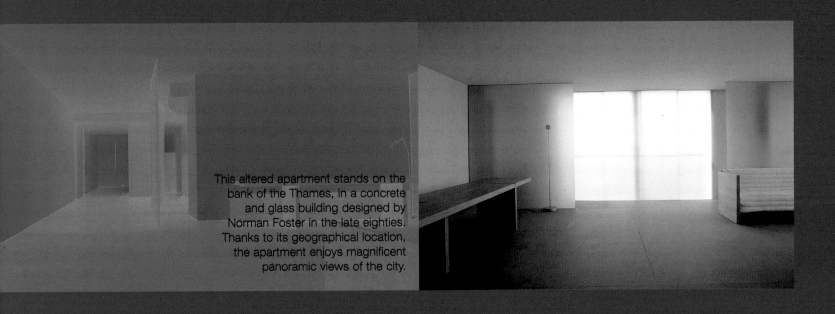

This altered apartment stands on the bank of the Thames, in a concrete and glass building designed by Norman Foster in the late eighties. Thanks to its geographical location, the apartment enjoys magnificent panoramic views of the city.

Silvestrin opened the north-south axis, flanked by a white, stylized wall, along which the city is projected uninterruptedly from one end of the apartment to the other. The flooring is of Tuscan Serena stone, the finish of which echoes the flow of the river.

Except for the chairs by Gio Ponti and others by Arne Jacobsen, the furniture was conceived by Silvestrin's studio. The sculptural lights built into the walls were designed by Adam Barker-Mill, the owner of the flat.

The bedrooms are separated from the daytime areas by a translucent screen that, although it subdivides the surface, reflects movement on both sides, creating a subtle, rather enigmatic effect. To the west, the openings of translucent glass both disseminate and protect the occupants from natural light.